The Limits of Organization

The Limits

of Organization

KENNETH J. ARROW

W · W · NORTON & COMPANY · INC · *NEW YORK*

ISBN 0 393 05507 8   CLOTH EDITION
ISBN 0 393 09323 9   PAPER EDITION

1 2 3 4 5 6 7 8 9 0

To the memory of my parents

Contents

Acknowledgments

The following were given as the Fels lectures for 1970–71, and I am indebted to The Fels Center of Government, and in particular to its Director, and my friend, Julius Margolis, not only for the opportunity but for encouraging a style of thought and presentation so different from my previous norm. The ideas developed here have drawn upon the thoughts of some of the outstanding thinkers of our time; my debt is inadequately acknowledged by the list of references at the end of this book.

Chapters 2 and 3 draw upon a paper, "The Agenda of Organization," prepared for a project on the role of the modern corporation in economic life in general and in innovation in particular undertaken by the Harvard University Program on Technology and Society. The paper is appearing as Chapter 7 in R. Marris and A. Wood (eds.), *The Corporate Economy: Growth, Competition, and Innovative Power*, London and Basingstoke: Macmillan, 1973. I wish to thank Dr. Emmanuel G. Mesthene, then Director of the Program, and Dr. Robin Marris, the project leader, for stimulating my interest and for permission to use the material.

The Limits of Organization

1

RATIONALITY: INDIVIDUAL AND SOCIAL

THE INTRICACIES and paradoxes in relations between the individual and his actions in the social context have been put very well by the great sage, Rabbi Hillel: "If I am not for myself, then who is for me? And if I am not for others, then who am I? And if not now, when?" Here we have, in three successive sentences, the essence of a tension that we all feel between the claims of individual self-fulfillment and those of social conscience and action. It is the necessity of every individual to express in some matters his intrinsic values. But the demands of society and the needs of the individual, expressed indeed only within that society, require that he be for others as well as for himself, that the others appear as ends to him as well as means. With two such questions with such different implications, it is no wonder we get to the third question: How can I behave urgently and with conviction when there are so many doubtful variables to contend with?

The tension between society and the individual is inevitable. Their claims compete within the individual conscience as well as in the arena of social conflict. There is no sense in which anybody lecturing or writing a huge book can come to a final resolution of these competing claims. All I try to insist here is that some sense of rational balancing of ends and means must be understood to play a major role in our understanding of ourselves and our social role. Let me illustrate by presenting or, more precisely, caricaturing some thought tendencies. We have one, loosely called "the new Left thought," not so new perhaps; some of us who have read a little bit of the history of thought have heard of anarchosyndicalism before. Bakunin and Sorel had spoken to the same point many years ago. But it is a real one. There is a demand for what might be termed sincerity, for a complete unity between the individual and the social roles, the notion that somehow in an ideal society there would be no conflict between one's demand on oneself and one's responses to the demands of society. It is true, of course, if you go back to Sorel, you would find mixed in with doctrines of this type the notion that these are also myths. This suggests that the resolution of conflict requires a certain restriction of our field of attention. The New Right, in its libertarian representatives, also resolves the conflict in its own way. It seeks to deny, or at least minimize, the role of the state and of collective action and responsibility, and substitutes for these claims, with their difficult moral and power consequences, the worship of the market. These are extremes. Most of us operate in some middle realm where we admit social claims, sometimes forget about them for long stretches of time as we go about in our daily private role, sometimes rise to an occasion, sometimes fall miserably short, as we assert our individuality in contexts that perhaps are not totally appropriate.

I want to discuss here the relation between society and the individual in, I would like to say a rational spirit, but let me be more particular, in the spirit of an economist. An economist by training thinks of himself as the guardian of rationality, the ascriber of rationality to others, and the prescriber of rationality to the social world. It is this role that I will play.

Why collective action? Why the need for having society, or at least for having it play significant economic roles? From the economist's point of view, it is because collective action can extend the domain of individual rationality. Collective action is a means of power, a means by which individuals can more fully realize their individual values. This point sounds trite at first blush, and for economists would hardly be worth a comment. It is more taken for granted than asserted. Nevertheless, it is not necessarily an agreeable point of view to those who may seek deeper emotional satisfaction from collective enterprises. Long ago, Edmund Burke said, "The age of chivalry is gone. That of sophisters, calculators, and economists has succeeded and the glory of Europe is extinguished for ever." The rather dry, recondite calculation of gains and losses does not lead to great enthusiasm. It does not offer magic resolutions to difficult problems. A truly rational discussion of collective action in general or in specific contexts is necessarily complex, and what is even worse, it is necessarily incomplete and unresolved. Rationality, after all, has to do with means and ends and their relation. It does not specify what the ends are. It only tries to make us aware of the congruence or dissonance between the two. So ultimately any value discussion must come to a rest temporarily on unanalyzed postulates. There is an infinite regress as we try to justify one value judgment in terms of supposedly deeper ones.

Let me briefly sketch what economists would look at in a question of choice, social or individual. Basically, we see an opposition or tension or equilibrium between two forces: values and opportunities. On the one hand, the individual has some meaningful sets of goals of all sorts or orders, from consumption of material goals to what we usually think of as higher goals, although perhaps these are not necessarily more important. But the possibility of realizing most goals is inherently limited. There is a restricted set of opportunities, among which the individual, acting by himself or through a collectivity of some kind, must choose. He must husband his scarce resources. He must choose among the opportunities available to him that one which best achieves his values.

The role of economist here is sometimes unpleasant. It's probably not entirely accidental, though a little unfair, that Carlyle referred to us as the practitioners of the dismal science. We frequently have to point out the limits of our opportunities. We have to say, "This or that, not both. You can't do both." What's worse, we have to point out frequently that the economic system is complex in its nature. It can easily happen that a step which on the face of it is an obvious way of achieving certain desired values may in fact frequently lead to their opposites. I cite, for example, many proposals for drastic increases in minimum wages. Surely we want to redistribute income to the lower end of the wage scale. The most obvious thing is to raise the wages. An economist realizes that the situation is not that simple, that the system can react to that policy; it does not passively accept it. The end result may be an increase in the volume of unemployment, an outcome worse than low wages. Of course, the role of the economist in pointing out limitations is not unique to him. It is the general role of the expert, and indeed there are other fields in which the obvious step is not necessarily the effective one. Recent research, for example, has suggested that when it comes to improving the quality of education, the obvious thing to do, simply pouring more resources into education along the current lines, is now expected to have very little effect.

These problems of values and opportunities arise even at the level of the single individual; even the isolated hunter or farmer, the Robinson Crusoe of our favorite textbook examples, has to face this kind of choice-problem. But what we are interested in here is the role of interpersonal relations in the organization of society. Starting from the economic viewpoint (though I think the situation is more general), it is clear that interpersonal relationships are needed as part of our collective organization, for our mutual improvement. They are needed for at least two reasons, although there are more. One is simply that the basic resources of the society, its natural resources, its human resources, its technological resources, are limited in supply, and the realization of alternative values or the attempts to find alternative activities for meeting those values imply a competition for these scarce resources. If we do things one way, we cannot do them another way. So we need to have a system which will mediate this competition, whether it be a market or an authoritative allocation system, as in the military or in the socialist state. We need, in any case, a social system of some complexity and of some considerable degree of organization in order to regulate the competition for resources, to allocate them among the different possible uses.

Further, interpersonal organization is needed to secure the gains that can accrue from cooperation. The essential considerations are two: (1) individuals are different and in particular have different talents, (2) individuals' efficiency in the performance of social tasks usually improves with specialization. We need cooperation to achieve specialization of function. This involves all the elements of trade and the division of labor. The blacksmith in the primitive village is not expected to eat horseshoes; he specializes in making horseshoes, the farmer supplies him with grain in exchange, and both (this is the critical point) can be made better off.

How do we evaluate alternative social organizations? There are many possible arrangements for meeting the needs of society and they satisfy many different needs. Some, however, are good, and some seem to be unsuccessful. At this moment I am not concerned with the achievement of a good society, but just with its definition. What do we mean by saying that one system is better than another? Again, for a commonplace of economic thought, we use the notion of efficiency or optimality that is associated with the name of Vilfredo Pareto. Whatever else we mean by better or efficient, we certainly mean the following: one situation, one system, or one allocation is better than another if every individual feels it is better according to his own individual values.

Surely, then, we do not want to accept a situation such that there is a better one than it according to this criterion. And so we speak of allocations or of systems as being *efficient* (I will use that simple term), when there is no other system or allocation which is better in this strong sense, which is better in the sense of making everybody better off. Now this definition is a very useful one for shearing away a lot of undesirable situations. It does not define, uniquely, a best situation in any sense of the word. If there are two individuals in our society, one of them can make individual A very well off indeed, individual B poorly off. The second one can do the opposite. Neither of those situations is strictly better that the other, according to our definition; they are simply incomparable. Other criteria—roughly speaking, those we associate with the term "distributive justice"—have to be called into play.

Now within this context, and under certain very special assumptions which I think would be unwise to elaborate on here for reasons of length, it is shown that efficiency can be achieved through a particular kind of social system, the price system..We allow our goods to be transferred through sale. Individuals derive their income by selling their services, their personal services and the services of things they own, at given prices. They use this income to purchase goods, again at these prices (in different amounts, doubtless, than they supply them). If, in fact, society's demands and supplies according to this arrangement are consistent with each other—that is, society is producing as an output neither more nor less than people want at these prices—then it is a fact, or it is a theorem (this may not be exactly the same thing), that the resulting state is efficient, providing certain hypotheses (which I am ignoring at the moment) are satisfied.

Furthermore, there are some real additional virtues to the system. Not only is it capable of achieving efficient allocations in the sense just described, but it requires of the participants in an economy relatively little knowledge. They need only know about their own needs. The individual need not worry about the social effects of his actions. According to the system, if he does something which affects somebody else, he pays the price. If he withdraws resources that somebody else could use, he is made aware through the price he has to pay, but he does not have to further consider the others as individuals. They are compensated through the prices he has to pay.

Further, not only do we have limited need for knowledge

(a man need only know the things he can be expected to know best) but, to put the same thing perhaps slightly differently, the individual has a sense of freedom. He is free to act within the system; there is no direct order telling him what to do. He has an income and he can spend it. Needless to say, this freedom of action is, from a certain point of view, somewhat illusory. It can be very small indeed if his income is very low. What one's income is, is not determined here by justice, but by a complicated system of interactions whose ethical meaning is hard to define. The idealization of freedom through the market completely ignores the fact that this freedom can be, to a large number of people, very limited in scope.

The price system can also be attacked on the grounds that it harnesses motives which our ethical systems frequently condemn. It makes a virtue of selfishness. Some economists, much taken with the system, have indeed argued that, for example, business corporations are committing a social wrong if they try to engage in socially desirable activities; that their aims should be properly only to maximize their profits, and that is indeed the socially most desirable activity they can engage in. This is a proposition for which there is some warrant in price theory, although it stretches the point rather considerably.

We are always disturbed by a system which relies completely on selfish motives. These motives are selfish in the strict, literal sense of the word. They pertain only to the individual; he, by definition, can ignore the rest of the world. Most of our ethical teachings certainly rather stress that we do not even want this sense of alienation and anonymity in our interpersonal relations. But true though that be, we must on the other hand not ignore the enormous gains in efficiency that can be achieved through the price system, as compared with most conceivable alternatives.

Nevertheless, there are profound difficulties with the price system, even, so to speak, within its own logic, and these strengthen the view that, valuable though it is in certain realms, it cannot be made the complete arbiter of social life. One point, and a difficult one indeed (it is one I have already alluded to) is that the price system does not in any way prescribe a just distribution of income. Given the way resources are distributed initially, including primarily human resources, abilities, training and the like, and also property, the system prescribes, through some very elaborate and indirect methods, how they are to be valued. There is no simple argument, and there are few economists, though perhaps many laymen, who would defend the proposition that there is a simple argument which states that the resulting distribution of income has any special claim to be called just. The price system then does not provide within itself any defensible income distribution, and this is a key drawback.

There are other drawbacks which can be discussed in a somewhat more objective way. In fact, in a strictly technical and objective sense, the price system does not always work. You simply cannot price certain things. A classical example that is usually used in textbooks and one of considerable importance, now become very fashionable, is the pollution of water or air. Hypothetically, to illustrate what a pure price system would be, someone would have to own the air, charge the polluter for the renting it out, that is, using it to carry the various poisons that our automobiles emit, and compensate those who suffer from the ill effects of pollution. I think it is clear that, speaking technically, we cannot police the boundary of the air. The enforcement of the price system in that context would be simply too difficult to achieve.

(It may be worth explaining why it would be better to charge prices for air pollution if it were possible to do so. By so doing, there is a strong inducement not to engage in pollution; and if the value of the polluting activity is sufficiently great so that it is not discouraged, at least the victims will be compensated.)

A similar difficulty in enforcing the price system is found

in the case of road use. The situation is not as extreme as in air pollution, since it is possible to impose tolls; but by and large, and most conspicuously in the case of urban roads, we understand that the sheer cost of trying to collect tolls would be much greater than the benefit in efficiency.

I am not interested here so much in these specific examples as to show that something like this occurs in more subtle contexts. Consider what is thought of as a higher or more elusive value than pollution or roads: trust among people. Now trust has a very important pragmatic value, if nothing else. Trust is an important lubricant of a social system. It is extremely efficient; it saves a lot of trouble to have a fair degree of reliance on other people's word. Unfortunately this is not a commodity which can be bought very easily. If you have to buy it, you already have some doubts about what you've bought. Trust and similar values, loyalty or truth-telling, are examples of what the economist would call "externalities." They are goods, they are commodities; they have real, practical, economic value; they increase the efficiency of the system, enable you to produce more goods or more of whatever values you hold in high esteem. But they are not commodities for which trade on the open market is technically possible or even meaningful.

It follows from these remarks that, from the point of view of efficiency as well as from the point of view of distributive justice, something more than the market is called for. Other modes of governing the allocation of resources occur. Most conspicuous among these is the government at all its levels. Government influences the allocation of resources by means that operate within the price system, but also otherwise. The government buys goods and services; that is still working through the price system. The government collects taxes, and taxes are not prices. They are not a voluntary exchange. The government of course also has its host of laws and regulations, coercive and certainly nonmarket methods of controlling and directing the economy and indeed society in general.

The government's role in internalizing externalities is then straightforward in principle, which does not imply that it is easy in practice. The signals it can use to recognize and measure those externalities it can deal with are necessarily imperfect, since these are precisely the areas in which the price system has failed to operate. The government may indeed perform somewhat better than the private sector in realizing social feelings, trust, and empathy, but within limits: power as well as money corrupts.

With regard to distributive justice, there are well known fundamental dilemmas in any concept of social good. Once an efficient allocation is reached, we have a situation of straight conflict. It is perfectly possible to defend the proposition that through one action or another (and we think here usually of taxation and redistribution), we can change the distribution of income as we wish, and then, after the redistribution, we can let a suitably corrected price system operate so as to assure efficient results. But of course we are here taking away from one and giving to another. We have a straight conflict situation, not one that can be resolved by integration, by jointly improving the welfare of each individual.

Scholars, both economists and writers on ethics, are trying to come to some kind of objective criteria. But I think that the search can be surely said to have been inconclusive for reasons that I think are intrinsic to the logic of the subject. The root facts here are the incommensurability and incomplete communicability of human wants and values. George Bernard Shaw long ago observed, "Do not do unto others as you would have that they do unto you. They may have different tastes." Social good, as in the determination of a just income distribution, is an abstraction of some kind from the individual values of the members of the society. But this abstraction can only be based on interpersonally observed behavior, as in market purchases or voting, not on the full range of an individual's feelings. As is by now well known, attempts to form social judgments by aggregating individual expressed preferences always lead to the possibility of paradox.

Thus there cannot be a completely consistent meaning to collective rationality. We have at some point a relation of pure power; and how the distribution is going to be resolved cannot be answered unequivocally, nor can we easily say that there are objectively valid ethical criteria. Some of the conflict, to be sure, is mitigated by the essential human feelings of sympathy. I am using the term here not with its usual rather debased and patronizing connotation, but in a more literal sense of feeling oneself to be in the other one's place. This motive operates with some, though doubtless inadequate, strength, and it clearly operates better in an institution, such as the government, designed to give some scope to expressing altruistic interests.

The government is, of course, only one of a large number of collective institutions. It is distinguished from the others primarily by its monopoly on coercive power, although even that monopoly is not absolute. A firm, especially a large corporation, provides another major area within which price relations are held in partial abeyance. The internal organization is again hierarchical and bureaucratic. Prices no doubt have powerful influences from the outside, and in many firms, at least, there are concerted attempts to simulate the operations of a hypothetical perfect market, perhaps even to do better than the sluggish and imperfectly informed markets of reality. But internally, and especially at lower levels, the relations among the employees of a firm are very different from the arm's length bargaining of our textbooks. As Herbert Simon has observed, an employment contract is different in many ways from an ordinary commodity contract; an employee is selling willingness to obey *authority*, a concept of central importance to which I will return in a later chapter. No doubt the employee is always free to leave, but since the costs of leaving are always present and frequently nontrivial, the employment relation creates an expectation of continued participation.

There are many other organizations beside the government and the firm. But all of them, whether political party or revolutionary movement, university or church, share the common characteristics of the need for collective action and the allocation of resources through nonmarket methods.

There is still another set of institutions, if that is the right word, I want to call to your attention and make much of. These are invisible institutions: the principles of ethics and morality. Certainly one way of looking at ethics and morality, a way that is compatible with this attempt at rational analysis, is that these principles are agreements, conscious or, in many cases, unconscious, to supply mutual benefits. The agreement to trust each other can not be bought, as I have said; it is not even necessarily very easy for it to be achieved by a signed contract saying that we will work with each other.

Societies in their evolution have developed implicit agreements to certain kinds of regard for others, agreements which are essential to the survival of the society or at least contribute greatly to the efficiency of its working. It has been observed, for example, that among the properties of many societies whose economic development is backward is a lack of mutual trust. Collective undertakings of any kind, not merely governmental, become difficult or impossible not only because A may betray B but because even if A wants to trust B he knows that B is unlikely to trust him. And it is clear that this lack of social consciousness is in fact a distinct economic loss in a very concrete sense, as well of course as a loss in the possible well-running of a political system. I approach this from the point of view of an economist so I speak of the failures of the price system; I am sure one could come to the same end from other points of view. But starting from this point of view, the fact that we cannot mediate all our responsibilities to others through prices, through paying for them, makes it essential in the running of society that we have what might be called "conscience," a feeling of responsibility for the effect of one's actions on others.

Unfortunately, this position cannot be pushed too far. We cannot know all the effects of our actions on all other people. When you take these obligations to others seriously you are forced into a very difficult position where you take actions whose consequences you cannot really know and yet you feel responsible for them. It is clear that at some point we must limit our sense of responsibility to others to have any effective action at all. As I have already sketched, the price system permits one extreme. We pay our debts, literally and figuratively, through prices, and we need not concern ourselves further about our responsibilities to others. Given that prices do not work completely (when we are on the open road we have some responsibility for endangering the lives of others, quite apart from any prices we may have to pay for it), we have to consider to some extent social responsibility, but then it has no simple, well-marked boundary.

It follows from the above kind of argument that at any moment an individual is necessarily faced with a conflict between his individual desires and the demands of society. I am therefore rejecting the view that there can be a complete unity, a complete identity of feeling between the social and individual contexts. One's social, one's political attitudes, for example, must always reflect a certain degree of compromise with one's individual point of view. The values you see at any one moment must be compromised because others see different values and no social action is possible at all without some element of cooperation and, in particular, agreement.

The demands of society sound like a formidable and crushing burden, but of course behind social rules are always other individual people and that is what we mean by accepting social demands, though the form may not always be obvious. Respect for the law, for example, looked at as a restriction on one's degree of freedom, seems bad. When one recalls that the law is, after all, the protection of other individuals' degree of freedom, the situation changes its form. But the others involved here frequently are abstractions. They are not people you know; they are not people that are concrete. Nevertheless, some sense of the individuals that may lie behind an abstraction must always be recognized.

Social demands may be expressed through formal rules and authorities, or they may be expressed through internalized demands of conscience. Looked at collectively, these demands may be compromises which are needed to increase the efficacy of all. At any moment they are apt to be felt by the individual as a set of shackles. And unfortunately there are still further problems. It may really be true that social agreements ultimately serve as obstacles to the achievement of desired values, even the values desired by all or by many. The problem is that agreements are typically harder to change than individual decisions. When you have committed not only yourself but many others to an enterprise, the difficulty of changing becomes considerable. If it is done on a conscious level, we have all the formalities involved in persuading others to change their minds. What may be hardest of all to change are unconscious agreements, agreements whose very purpose is lost to our minds. Some commitments are to purposes which involve much sacrifice and very great depth of involvement. A commitment to a war or a revolution or to religion is typically one that is very hard to reverse, even if conditions have changed from the time when the thing started. Even if experience has shown the unexpectedly undesirable consequences of a commitment, the past may continue to rule the present. In one of the early books of the *Iliad*, Agamemnon raises the question whether the Greeks should not abandon the siege of Troy. They had been there for nine years; they hadn't gotten anywhere; many brave men had died. Perhaps it is implicit that the war started over a woman who wasn't worthy of all this. Of course, Agamemnon is raising all these arguments not because he believes them but because he intends to persuade the Greeks to stay. Odysseus makes them realize this is all quite irrelevant. What is really important is that they would be breaking their commitment; therefore they must stay and fight the war.

It is this thinking which I think gives rise to the greatest tragedies of history, this sense of commitment to a past purpose which reinforces the original agreement precisely at a time when experience has shown that it must be reversed.

I have made a number of points and I think I have succeeded in contradicting myself on most of them, showing both sides. And if I can do this in an abstract discussion, I can do it much more readily if I take any concrete social problem and expose the multisidedness of it, the consequences to others that we do not see, to those who are yet to come. "If not now, when?" Ho do we talk about action in this context?

Rationality and foresight are indeed capable of creating delay and doubt; so, too, are conscience, respect for others, the sense of vague respect to distant and unforeseen consequences that we may worry about. The True Believer is much more effective in social action, but whether it is in the right direction may be another question. "The native hue of resolution/Is sicklied over with the pale cast of thought." There are no simple answers here and I am not going to give any. There are moments of history when we simply must act, fully knowing our ignorance of possible consequences, but to retain our full rationality we must sustain the burden of action without certitude, and we must always keep open the possibility of recognizing past errors and changing course.

2

ORGANIZATION AND INFORMATION

IN THE LAST CHAPTER, I took the viewpoint that organizations are a means of achieving the benefits of collective action in situations in which the price system fails.

I am not going to attempt a formal definition of organizations, which would probably be impossible. Rather the concept is really a primitive term in a system, its significance being revealed by assumptions and their consequences. As noted in the last lecture, the term, "organization," should be interpreted quite broadly. Formal organizations, firms, labor unions, universities, or government, are not the only kind. Ethical codes and the market system itself are to be interpreted as organizations; the market system, indeed, has elaborate methods for communication and joint decision-making. As this example makes clear, the participants in organizations may be themselves organizations as well as individuals. Furthermore, it is important to note that individuals typically belong to many organizations.

The purpose of organizations is to exploit the fact that many (virtually all) decisions require the participation of many individuals for their effectiveness. In particular, as noted last time, organizations are a means of achieving the benefits of collective action in situations in which the price system fails.

There is one particular failure of the price system to which I want to stress, one that is absolutely central to the understanding of organizations. I refer to the presence of uncertainty. Now there is a purely theoretical device for introducing the price system to handle uncertainty in certain aspects. Since this approach may not be familiar to all, it may be as well to sketch it here.

Uncertainty means that we do not have a complete description of the world which we fully believe to be true. Instead, we consider the world to be in one or another of a range of states. Each state of the world is a description which is complete for all relevant purposes. Our uncertainty consists in not knowing which state is the true one. The uncertainty may be about conditions of production or tastes or anything else which, if known, would affect individuals' desires to trade. Then instead of contracts to buy and sell fixed amounts of goods, it would be better to have conditional contracts, or contracts in *contingent commodities*, to use the technical term, that is, each unit contract is for the delivery of a one unit of some good *if* a specified state has occurred. Since the state of the world completely specifies demand and supply conditions, it is possible to prescribe that contingent contracts can always be carried out, since we need offer to deliver exactly as much would be available in the state which the contract is contingent. Prices can be attached to these contracts; then the standard theory of the competitive economy without uncertainty can be reinterpreted to give a theory of competitive equilibrium under uncertainty. A commodity in the ordinary sense is replaced by a contingent commodity.

From this account, it can be seen that this theoretical scheme has some parallels in the real world. Insurance policies exist; so does the necessary evil of the cost-plus contract. Much more important, the common stock market serves for the diffusion of risks. But clearly also the range of contingencies for which conditional contracts are available is much more limited than would be ideally desirable in theory. The taking of desirable economic risks is inhibited by the inability to insure against business failure, for example. At a more detailed level, the coordination of complicated production processes within a firm is in part a question of uncertainty— for example, random delays in one part or another of the process. One could imagine a price system in principle for internal coordination of the firms: the department which supplies a part to another would sell it at a price which varies according to the average length of the delay. The selling department would have a clear incentive to reduce the delay. However, the risks to the buyer can be optimally allocated only if there is a system of insurance against the contingencies which can create delays; otherwise, the buying department would have to alter the scope of its operations so as to minimize uncertainty, an alteration which would result in reduced output overall. It is not hard to see that such a combination of prices and insurance would be exceedingly difficult to implement in practice.

There is more than one reason for the failure of the theoretically desirable contingent prices to exist. One doubtless is the sheer complexity of the price schedule. An insurance policy would have to specify an enormous number of contingencies with, in general, different payments for each possibility. Drawing up such contracts would be expensive, and understanding them equally so. The courts of law, on the basis of long experience, have shown little faith in the ability of the average individual to understand complicated contracts. An illustration is the treatment of the so-called exculpatory clauses. For example, when shipping goods, the transportation company frequently includes in its contract a clause exempting it from liability for damage to or loss of the goods shipped. Formally, one could regard this simply as determining the locus of risk-bearing. Once this is determined, a perfect market could permit the reshifting of risks, for example, through insurance. But courts have consistently refused to enforce such clauses and have held the transport companies liable anyway. Their argument is that it is too much to expect the average shipper, who is small compared with the transport company, to appreciate the risks in question.

Another major reason for limitation of the price system for allocating risk-bearing is the difficulty of distinguishing between genuine risks and failures to optimize, a difficulty referred to by students of insurance as *moral hazard*. For example, the outbreak of a fire may be due to a combination of exogenous circumstances and individual choice, such as carelessness or, in the extreme case, arson. Hence, a fire insurance policy creates an incentive for an individual to change his behavior and ceases to be a pure insurance against an uncontrollable event.

Roy Radner has put the matter in more general perspective by observing the key role of information in the possibility of arriving at contingent contracts. Briefly, my sketch of the pure theory of allocation of risk-bearing has implicitly assumed that all individuals know what state of nature prevails when the contracts are finally fulfilled, when the insurance payments are made. It suffices, to be precise, that they will have the same information, whatever it may be. But in most cases, this will not be so. To illustrate, consider the problem known in insurance literature as *adverse selection*. The insured may know his risks better than the insurer, for example, in life insurance. The insurer may start by choosing his rates on some actuarial basis. But then the high-risk groups will buy more of the insurance than the average, while the low-risk groups will buy less. Hence, the experience of the insurer, as weighted by dollars, will be less favorable than the actuarial. The rates will have to be raised, but this will drive still more of the low-risk groups out. Clearly a situation will be created in which there are many whose risks are inadequately covered, because it is not known how low those risks really are. The essential cause is an inequality of information between the two parties to the contract.

Another illustration of the inequality of information among economic agents is the relation between patient and physician. It is of the essence of this or other relations between principal and agent that they differ in their information about the world. But this means that there can really be no contract which insures against the agent's failure to do his business properly. I have argued in a study of medical economics that one might regard professional ethics as an example of an institution which fills in some measure the gap created by the corresponding failure of the price system.

It follows that the information structure of individual economic agents powerfully conditions the possibilities of allocating risk-bearing through the market. By information structure here I mean not merely the state of knowledge existing at any moment of time but the possibility of acquiring relevant information in the future. We speak of the latter in communication terminology as the possession of an *information channel*, and the information to be received as *signals* from the rest of the world.

Thus the possibility of using the price system to allocate uncertainty, to insure against risks, is limited by the structure of the information channels in existence. Put the other way, the value of nonmarket decision-making, the desirability of creating organizations of a scope more limited than the market as a whole, is partially determined by the characteristics of the network of information flows.

But the presence or absence of information channels is not prescribed exogenously to the economic system. Channels can be created or abandoned, and their capacities and the types of signals to be transmitted over them are subject to choice, a choice based on a comparison of benefits and costs. I therefore turn to an examination of the characteristics of information and in particular some generalities on the benefits and costs of information channels. In the next chapter, I will discuss more specifically the organization as a processor of information.

Each individual economic agent is assumed to start with the ability to receive some signals from the natural and social environments. This capacity is not, however, unlimited, and the scarcity of information-handling ability is an essential feature for the understanding of both individual and organizational behavior. The individual also starts off with a set of expectations as to the range of signals that he or anybody else might possibly receive now or in the future and probabilities of receiving the different signals. In technical terms, the individual begins with a prior probability distribution over the space of possible signals. The concept of signal is to be interpreted broadly; some signals might inform the individual of the outcome of his decisions, some might be used as the basis of decisions, if only of implicit decisions not to act. A signal is then any event capable of altering the individual's probability distribution; in more technical language, the posterior distribution of signals conditional on the observation of one may, in general, differ from the prior. This transformation of probabilities is precisely what constitutes the acquisition of information.

This definition of information is qualitative, and so it will remain for the purposes of this volume. The quantitative definition which appears in information theory is probably of only limited value for economic analysis, for reasons pointed out by Marschak; different bits of information, equal from the viewpoint of information theory, will usually have very different benefits or costs. Thus, let A and B be any two statements about the world, for neither of which is its truth or falsity known *a priori*. Then a signal that A is true conveys exactly as much information, in the sense of Shannon, as a statement that B is true. But the value of knowing whether or not A is true may be vastly greater than the value of knowing B's truth-value; or it may be that the resources needed to ascertain the truth-value of A are much greater than those for B. In either case, the information-theoretic equivalence of the two possible signals conceals their vast economic difference.

The channels initially open to the individual may be augmented by the creation of new channels. The choice of new channels will be determined by their benefits and costs. There is little that one can say systematically about the benefits for information in general. The main remark that can be ventured on now is the familiar one that there are increasing returns to the *uses* of information. The same body of technological information, for example, can be used in production on any scale and therefore towards productive enterprises with some degree of monopoly power, in accordance with familiar principles.

Let us now turn to the costs of information, that is, to the inputs needed for the installation and operation of information channels. First and most important, the individual himself is an input, indeed the chief input if quantification is at all meaningful here, into any of his information channels. Immediately or ultimately, the information must enter his brain through his sensory organs, and both brain and senses are limited in capacity. Information may be accumulated in files, but it must be retrieved to be of use in decision-making. The psychological literature has many studies of the limits on the sensory perception abilities of human beings and some on their limits as information-processors. I do not want to argue for fixed coefficients in information-handling any more than in more conventional production activities; substitution of other factors, especially computers, for the individual's mind is possible. But the individual's very limited capacity for acquiring and using information is a fixed factor in information processing, and one may expect a sort of diminishing returns to increases in other information resources. Organization theorists have long recognized limits of this kind under the heading of "span of control."

A second key characteristic of information costs is that they are in part capital costs; more specifically, they typically represent an irreversible investment. I am not placing much weight on the physical aspects of communication, telephone lines and the like, though they are in fact non-negligible in cost and they do provide a concrete, understandable paradigm. Rather I am thinking of the need for having made an adequate investment of time and effort to be able to distinguish one signal from another. Learning a foreign language is an obvious example of what I have in mind. The subsequent ability to receive signals in French requires this initial investment. There are in practice many other examples of codes that have to be learned in order to receive messages; the technical vocabulary of any science is a case in point. The issue here is that others have found it economical to use one of a large number of possible coding methods, and for any individual it is necessary to make an initial investment to acquire it.

However, even when the codes are not deliberately contrived, there is a need for an initial attempt at understanding. The empirical scientist in any area has to make preliminary observations (or learn them from others, which also involves an investment) in order to read nature's signals. Similarly, as E. H. Gombrich has emphasized, our understanding of a particular school of art, and indeed the understanding by artists themselves, depends on a degree of familiarity with it. Thus, there tends to be a cycle in which an innovation in artistic vision first occurs and is diffused; then, as it becomes more familiar, the value of repetition of similar signals decreases, and the ability to understand new signals, i.e., departures from the new tradition, increases.

One might attempt to formalize the capital aspect of information in this way. A signal hitherto unheard is useless by itself; it does not modify any probability distribution. However, a preliminary sampling experiment in which the relation between the new signal and more familiar ones can be determined or at least estimated will serve to make valuable further signals of the new type. This experiment, which may be vicarious (education, scientific literature), is an act of investment.

Such investment, being locked up in an individual's mind, is necessarily irreversible. It can of course be transmitted to others, but it remains in the possession of the individual and cannot be alienated by him, though, like most irreversible investments, it is subject to depreciation.

In the last twenty years, there has developed some theoretical literature on irreversible investment. Obviously irreversibility is of no consequence when the future is one of steadily growing demand for the capital good; but it becomes of importance when there are fluctuations, particularly stochastic fluctuations. Now by its very nature the value of an information channel is uncertain, and so we have an economic problem which resembles the demand for inventories under conditions of uncertainty. We may venture on some possible generalizations. One is that the demand for investment in information is less than it would be if the value of the information were more certain. The second, most important I would guess, is that the random accidents of history will play a bigger role in the final equilibrium. Once the investment has been made and an information channel acquired, it will be cheaper to keep on using it than to invest in new channels, especially since the scarcity of the individual as an input, already alluded to, implies that the use of new channels will diminish the product of old ones. Thus, it will be difficult to reverse an initial commitment in the direction in which information is gathered. Even if the expected value of the difference between two possible channels was relatively small and even if subsequent information suggested that the initial choice was wrong, it would not pay to reverse the decision later on.

A third basic characteristic of information costs is that they are by no means uniform in different directions. At any given moment an individual is a bundle of abilities and accumulated information. He may easily find it cheaper to open certain information channels rather than others in ways connected with these abilities and this knowledge. Thus, an explorer in hitherto unknown territory will find it easier to explore new areas near to those he has already covered. Geographical propinquity is but a special case. It is cheaper to proceed to the chemical analysis of compounds similar to those already studied. Learning generalizes naturally and cheaply in some directions, with much greater difficulty in others. A rat shocked at one point will generalize by staying some distance away; the avoidance effect falls off with distance.

It is also easier to communicate with other individuals with whom one has a common approach or a common language, literally or metaphorically. The capital accumulation of learning a code, referred to earlier, may have to be engaged in at both ends of the channel. In the usual economic analysis, known as the theory of the core, collusive agreements in an industry are not stable because there always exist alternative allocative deals involving some producers and some consumers which are preferable from the viewpoint of the participants. But if, as Adam Smith once suggested, members of the same trade find it easy to communicate with each other, presumably because of their common experiences, it may well be that the exchange of information leading to a collusive agreement among producers of one commodity is much cheaper than that needed to achieve a blocking coalition. Hence, the collusive agreement may in fact be stable. (The concept of class interest and identification may be related to ease of communication among individuals with similar life experiences.)

The relative costs of communication channels may also be influenced by activities of the individual other than the collection of information. There is a complementary between a productive activity and some kinds of information. An individual cannot help making observations while working at some task. These observations are signals which in some circumstances change his knowledge about this productive activity, so-called learning by doing. In other circumstances, they may yield information relevant in other, seemingly remote, areas of decision-making, a phenomenon known as serendipity. We are all familiar with the accomplishments of explorers who were seeking the Northwest Passage.

To sum up, the costs of information, in the general sense of utilization of scarce resources, (a) are in some sense increasing for the individual because he is himself a scarce input, (b) involve a large irreversible capital element, and (c) vary in different directions.

In the next chapter I will discuss more specifically the role of information channels within an organization, to illustrate and amplify the cost propositions developed today in this context, and to examine in a general way the implications for the process and outcome of organizational decision-making.

3

THE AGENDA
OF ORGANIZATIONS

IN CLASSICAL maximizing theory it is implicit that the values of all relevant variables are at all moments under consideration. All variables are therefore *agenda* of the organization, that is, their values have always to be chosen. On the other hand, it is a commonplace of everyday observation and of studies of organization that the difficulty of arranging that a potential decision variable be recognized as such may be much greater than that of choosing a value for it. What the Federal Government regards as appropriate agenda has changed rapidly; nor can it be maintained that the new agenda necessarily correspond to changes in demand or supply, i.e., the emergence of new problems in the world or of new techniques for their solution. Unemployment insurance is an old idea, and the need for it did not emerge only in the Great Depression; but it suddenly changed from a nonagendum to an agendum. Similar examples can be cited for all sorts of organizations; innovation by firms is in many cases simply a question of putting an item on its agenda before other firms do. We can also see some items now in the process of arriving on the agenda. In the case of the Federal Government, the possibility of flexible exchange rates is at least on the horizon.

On the other hand, there is clearly a real value to putting an item on the agenda. The Employment Act of 1946 amounted to nothing more than a statement that full employment was at last on the Federal agenda, and many felt that this was a hollow victory indeed. But those who opposed it so violently were not deceived; in the long run, this recognition was decisive, though the process of implementing the responsibility was slow indeed. Once an item has arrived on the agenda, it is difficult not to treat it in a somewhat rational manner, if this is at all possible, and almost any considered solution may be better than neglect. I hasten to add that this generalization has its exceptions; there are problems for which there are no satisfactory solutions; placing such an item on the agenda may create a demand for a solution, which will of necessity be unsatisfactory. Thus there is some justification for the principle of "salutory neglect," but on the whole this exception is not likely to be real. An unsatisfactory solution may be what is needed to provoke the needed information-gathering to produce a better one, while neglect is never productive.

I want to sketch here some thoughts on the factors determining agenda. This problem already exists for the individual, and some time will be first devoted to him. But it will be suggested that the nature and purpose of organizations create additional implications for the determination of agenda and, in particular, for sluggishness in the introduction of new items.

What will be presented is not, strictly speaking, a theory or model but the kinds of considerations that will or should enter into a formulation of such a model. There does not seem to be great difficulty in formalizing the concepts to be presented, though handling them analytically to produce strong implications may be very difficult indeed. But at this stage it seemed more appropriate to raise these questions in a broad way, to avoid concentration on analytic problems. The point of view is that of an optimizing model but in a rich framework of uncertainty and information channels. Decisions, wherever taken, are a function of information received; then when information remains unchanged, no decision is made, or, to put the matter in a slightly more precise way, the implicit decision is made not to change the values of certain variables. In turn, the acquisition of information must be analyzed, since it is itself the result of decisions.

Of course, it is essential to this argument that information is scarce or costly; it can be assumed that any free information is acquired. As will be argued, the fact that for any given individual or organization different sorts of information have different costs has many implications for organizational behavior.

The theme to be presented is that the combination of uncertainty, indivisibility, and capital intensity associated with information channels and their use imply (a) that the actual structure and behavior of an organization may depend heavily upon random events, in other words on history, and (b) the very pursuit of efficiency may lead to rigidity and unresponsiveness to further change.

Decisions are necessarily a function of information. Hence, if it is decided to collect no information relevant to a certain class of decisions, those decisions are nonagenda.

The last sentence, by its uses of the words, "decided," and, "decision," highlights the need for a distinction between two kinds of decisions, decisions to act in some concrete sense, and decisions to collect information. The distinction is very familiar in statistical decision theory; the two are referred to as "terminal acts" and "experiments," respectively, by Raiffa and Schlaifer in their standard work. A prototypical illustration occurs in what is known as acceptance sampling. A firm or government is buying large quantities of some good. The quality of the good may vary from item to item. A typical procedure, when a lot of goods arrives, is to take a sample, test each item in it, and accept or reject the entire lot on the basis of the results in the sample. The sampling and testing constitute an experiment in this sense, the decision to accept or reject is the terminal act. If the cost of testing is at all considerable, it will be much cheaper, on the average, to test a sample than to test every item in the lot. Both the experiment and the terminal act are relevant to resource utilization. The experiment has implications for resource utilization because it is costly, the terminal act because it is a decision which may be beneficial or not. The experiment yields no benefits directly, but it has the instrumental value of improving the terminal act by supplying more information.

If the resource effects of the two steps are additive, the distinction between experiments and terminal acts can be held to rigorously. Even though this additivity is not always valid, it is suggestive.

Suppose we imagine that there are a number of different decision areas for the organization within each of which we have a range of possible experiments and a range of possible terminal acts. Suppose further these decision areas are sufficiently independent so that the values of terminal acts in the different areas are more or less additive. A decision area may be *active, monitored,* or *passive.* An active area is one in which experiments are performed, signals received from them, and terminal acts chosen as functions of the signals. A monitored area is one in which some experiments are being performed; the signals received convey too little information to take terminal acts, but if appropriate signals are received, it is optimal to make further experiments, which in turn will yield enough information to bring the terminal acts onto the agenda. Finally, a passive area is one in which no experiments are being conducted, and therefore neither experiments nor terminal acts are on the agenda.

The partition of decision areas among these types will depend of course on the relative benefits and costs. There is a little that can be said in a general way about anticipated benefits, but the classification of information costs in the last chapter may have some explanatory power. As an illustration, consider an individual investor choosing a portfolio of securities. There will be one class of securities in which the individual is actively investing; he has positive investments in them or else they are being watched closely, with the decision to invest or not invest being thought about steadily. The investor will be watching the market prices, receiving reports on the activities of the firms, and so forth. There will be a second class of securities which he is watching, so to speak, out of the corner of his eye. He occasionally checks prices and looks at relatively cursory information. If interesting movements or other information appears, he may increase the intensity of his surveillance and move the security into the active group. Finally, he will pay no attention whatever to the largest number of securities.

Analysis of information costs suggests some systematic reasons for classifying securities into one group or another. Familiarity with a particular firm or industry, because of previous experiences or current productive relations, will mean that information about some securities will be cheaper than about others; the investor has a background which enables him to understand the signals better. The fact that information has a strong capital component means that once an investor has chosen a selected list of securities, he will stay within that group, because additional information about the same securities is cheaper than acquiring the initial information about other securities needed to begin meaningful analysis.

He is likely to monitor securities for which some information is cheap because its acquisition is complementary to other activities. Thus, as a background for analysis of the securities he is primarily interested in, he may pick up some information about others; from the point of view of the latter group, this process amounts to inexpensive monitoring. Professional information services, brokers and the like, may supply him with broadly spread, if shallow information, at the same time they supply detailed information. General news sources about business conditions may be read simply because of their intrinsic interest and hence at virtually no cost; but these may constitute a certain amount of monitoring. Finally, simply social associations with business connections may constitute a source of information, the stronger because much evidence shows that personal influences are regarded as more reliable, which means that they convey more information, subjectively measured, at a given cost.

How then do we expect the agenda of an individual to change, that is, how do decision areas get changed from one

class to another? The monitoring process is a built-in explanation of part of the process. There are a lot of potential decision areas which are in fact being looked at a little bit. A
classical illustration of monitoring is the process of quality
control in industry. The quality of the product is tested on
a sampling basis. So long as the results are satisfactory, nothing is done; but when deterioration occurs, there is a more
thorough investigation of its causes, with the possible eventuality that a machine is repaired or replaced. But clearly there
is more to the matter than agenda changes as the result of
foreseen possibilities. One possibility is a sharp change in
payoffs to terminal acts. In particular, the opportunity benefit, that is the change in benefits due to a change in action,
may rise because of a decrease in the return to the present,
unexamined, action. In plain language, we have a "crisis." In
William James's term, a "coercive fact" may be more persuasive than any speculation about potential benefits from
change. The sinking of the *Titanic* led to iceberg patrols.

No doubt the changes in payoffs may be changes in perceptions rather than in actuality. The current ecological concerns have grown much more rapidly than the actual problems (which is not to say that they are not important; they
are). What sometimes happens is that the cost of signals goes
down, for one of many reasons. There may simply be a threshold effect; beyond a certain point, the effects of, say, pollution or the low performance of our portfolio, become obvious
with virtually no investment in observation or experiment. In
some cases, it may be that some other individuals, for their
own reasons, are supplying signals cheaply. These are the
reformers and agitators of all sorts; no doubt, their work only
flourishes when the value and cost structures are appropriate,
but the torch, though ready, still has to be lit by someone.

Another cause of agenda changes is that information
channels do not, despite the model that has been tentatively
used, stand in a simple relation to the partition of decision
areas which has been assumed above. Signals with quite dif-

ferent policy implications may be closely interrelated in origin and be received over the same channel; or it may be that an experiment for one purpose can yield a additional information relevant to very different terminal acts with only slightly additional cost. An interesting paradigm is that of opportunistic replacement; when a complex mechanism, such as a missile, is being examined to check for possible malfunctioning of one subunit, it becomes much cheaper to examine or replace others.

Let us turn to the factors determining the agenda of organizations. As noted earlier, the functional role of organizations is to take advantage of the superior productivity of joint actions. In the discussion of the internal economies of the firm, this point is of course customary with regard to what has been here called terminal acts. But it is equally and even more valid with regard to experiments, that is, information channels.

An organization can acquire more information than any one individual, for it can have each member performing different experiments. Thus, the limitations on an individual's capacity are overcome. But as always there is a price to be paid. In fact, the relevant considerations have been adduced in some of the old discussions of the U-shaped cost curve. The information has to be coordinated if it is to be of any use to the organization. More formally stated, communication channels have to be created within the organization.

Now if all information received by any member of the organization were transmitted to all others or even to one headquarters, there would be no gain in information processing costs. Indeed, there would be a loss, since there are additional information channels within the firm. The economies of information in the organization occur because in fact much of the information received is irrelevant. The terminal acts within the competence of the organization do not require for assessment the entire probability distribution of states of the world but only some marginal distributions derived from it. Hence, in general, the information received by a member of the organization can be transformed into a much smaller volume for retransmission without losing value for choice of terminal acts. The theory of sufficient statistics is an example of this reduction of information without loss of value. In this case, the reason is that the value of any terminal act depends only on the parameters of the underlying distribution and not on the values observed in the sample; hence it suffices to transmit the values of a function of the sample which exhausts its information about the parameters.

It is this reduction in retransmission which explains the utility of an organization for information-handling. Since information is costly, it is clearly optimal, in general, to reduce the internal transmission still further. That is, it pays to have some loss in value for the choice of terminal act in order to economize on internal communication channels. The optimal choice of internal communication structures is a vastly difficult question. It underlies, not always explicitly, the great controversies on the economics of socialism and has received deep exploration in certain directions in the Marschak-Radner theory of teams.

Since it is, in general, optimal not to transmit all the relevant information, an individual member will have accumulated information which is not under present circumstances judged worthwhile to transmit. It is possible that at a later time this information will turn out to be of value, due to receipt of some other signal which is complementary to it. Whether this information will then be used depends on a number of factors; among them are the cheapness of transmission over time, by means of memory or files and subsequent retrieval. This creates the possibility that different members of the organization who have had different experiences which have not been transmitted will interpret new signals in different ways. There seem to be interesting implications for a reduction of informational efficiency in organizations whose external environment has changed considerably.

Since internal communication channels can be designed, their structure can be chosen with a view to cost minimization. In particular, the efficiency of a channel can be increased by suitable choice of a code. This term is used both literally and metaphorically. It refers to all the known ways, whether or not inscribed in formal rules, for conveying information. As is well known from information theory, the optimal code will depend upon the *a priori* distribution of possible signals, as well as upon the costs of communicating differingly coded signals.

The role of coding has two economic implications: (1) it weakens but does not eliminate the tendency to increasing costs with scale of operation; (b) it creates an intrinsic irreversible capital commitment of the organization. With regard to the first point, we have seen that the organization's gains from increasing scale are derived by having its members make different experiments, that is, by specialization. As we have seen in the last chapter's discussion of the economics of information for the individual, this means the members will be accumulating differing types of skills in information-processing, learning (acquiring capital) in the areas in which they are specializing and unlearning elsewhere. As a result, communication among them becomes more difficult (as academic specialists are learning), and the codes used in their intercommunications have to become more complex. Hence, while coding permits a greater number of individual information sources to be pooled usefully, there are still increasing costs eventually as the scale of operations grows.

With regard to the second point, we have already argued that the learning of a code by an individual is an act of irreversible investment for him. It is therefore also an irreversible capital accumulation for the organization. It follows that organizations, once created, have distinct identities, because the costs of changing the code are those of unanticipated obsolescence.

Becker and others have stressed that a significant part of

accumulation of human capital consists of training specific to the needs of a firm, an input of information to the worker which increases his value to the firm but not to other firms. If the function of labor is to cooperate in production with capital goods which are held widely by different firms, it would appear that virtually all training is general. But learning the information channels within a firm and the codes for transmitting information through them is indeed a skill of value only internally.

One might ask, as one does frequently in the theory of the firm, why all firms do not have the same codes, so that training in the code is transferable? In the first place, in this combinatorial situation, there may easily be many optimal codes, all equally good, but to be useful in a firm it is important to know the right code. The situation here is very much that of the games of coordination which have been stressed so much by Schelling. If it is valuable for two people to meet without being able to communicate with each other during their trips, the meeting-place must be agreed on beforehand. It may not matter much where the meeting is to be. But a person who learned one meeting-place is not much use to an organization which has selected another.

In the second place, history matters. The code is determined in accordance with the best expectations at the time of the firm's creation. Since the code is part of the firm's or more generally the organization's capital, as already argued, the code of a given organization will be modified only slowly over time. Hence, the codes of organizations starting at different times will in general be different even if they are competitive firms. Indeed, individuals starting firms at the same time may well have different *a priori* distributions and therefore different codes.

The need for codes mutually understandable within the organization imposes a uniformity requirement on the behavior of the participants. They are specialized in the information capable of being transmitted by the codes, so that, in a process already described, they learn more in the direction of their activity and become less efficient in acquiring and transmitting information not easily fitted into the code. Hence, the organization itself serves to mold the behavior of its members.

This process may well have interesting implications for the behavior of the organization. The code of the organization may be supposed governed most strongly by its primary functions. But an organization has in general many functions, auxiliary indeed to its primary ones but important to its welfare. Alternatively, it may be thought desirable to add some secondary functions to the organization because their accomplishment appears to be complementary to the primary ones. But if the code appropriate to the primary functions is inappropriate to the auxiliary or secondary functions, the organization may function badly. Burton Klein has provided one illustration in an unpublished manuscript: the primary function of the military is the coordination of large masses of men and material in circumstances where coordination is according to a previously planned timetable. Research and development on military weapons is, in the present era, an important auxiliary service. But, Klein has argued, it tends to be run by men who think in military terms and therefore expect coordination of achievements at predictable time points in the future. In fact, of course, research and development are prime examples of information-gathering with a considerable degree of uncertainty, and achievements are certainly not predictable. As a result the precisely laid-out timetables are dramatically unfulfilled, as Summers has shown. The costs in the end are much higher than they would have been if the uncertainty had been taken into account initially. Klein's recommended solution, indeed, is to remove military research and development from military control and put it in the hands of a separate civilian agency.

An example of the difficulty of adding functions to an existing organization is provided by the tendency to add man-

agement control functions to existing accounting and budgetary departments. Since the quantitative basis of scientific
decision-making overlaps so heavily with classical accounts,
it is appealing to economize by joining the two functions.
But in fact the purposes differ considerably and therefore the
code, the way of looking at the world, differs also. The ac-
countant, whose aim is in part to insure against dishonesty,
is interested in a degree of precision in certain data unnecessary for management science but not interested in other
and rougher kinds of data. Budgetary control is also different
in many ways from scientific management, and some students
of public administration are highly critical of the recent ad-
dition of management control to the functions of the former
Bureau of the Budget.

Because of these difficulties of communication, there has
been in both the public and private sectors a tendency to hive
off incompatible functions into new organizations. Stigler has
pointed suggestively to the steady vertical disintegration
which has accompanied the growth of large firms; the forces
of the market make it profitable for the specialization in auxiliary services. Similarly, in the government, Franklin D.
Roosevelt seems to have been the innovator who first saw the
need of assigning new tasks to new bureaus, even though
according to some logic it belonged in the sphere of an existing department.

Let us return to the original purpose of this chapter, the
determination of the agenda of organizations. Basically, the
possible causes of changes in the agenda of organizations are
the same as those of individuals: a signal may be received
in a monitored area on the basis of which it is judged worthwhile to make the area active; the payoffs to terminal acts
may change or may be perceived to change abruptly; or an
information channel used primarily for one purpose may turn
up a signal with implications for taking action in a hitherto
passive area. The discussion of organizations just concluded
has been directed towards expanding the cost factors specific

to organizations which change the bases on which organizations change their agenda. In many ways, indeed, the costs of change may be greater for an organization. More exactly, it has a greater ability to monitor but a lesser ability to change from a passive attitude to a monitoring or active role.

There is one effect on organization which has no parallel in individuals. An organization is typically composed of changing individuals. Now any individual typically has access to many communication channels, of which this particular organization is only one. In particular, education is such a channel. Thus, the organization is getting the benefit of a considerable amount of information which is free to it. Even though the code of the organization may make the internal transmission of such information costly, if there is enough of it, the behavior of the organization will change. In particular, new items will appear on the organization's agenda. If we think of education as the primary source of new information, then it is introduced into an organization by its youngest and newest members. Thus we have the possibility of changes in organizational agenda induced by generational changes. More generally, the prime need in organizational design is increasing capacity to handle a large agenda. To the extent that information and its handling are accumulations of personal capital, what is needed is what Pareto called the "circulation of elites," the turnover of decision-makers. More generally, what is needed is a "circulation of information and decision rules." Shortrun efficiency and even flexibility within a narrow frameworks of alternatives may be less important in the long run than a wide compass of potential activities. These are some of the considerations in the design of public and private organizations and the choice between them in carrying out the tasks of society.

4

AUTHORITY AND RESPONSIBILITY

1. A conflict of goals

AMONG THE MOST widespread characteristics of organizations is the prevalence of authoritative allocation. Virtually universally, in organizations of any size, decisions are made by some individuals and carried out by others. The fields in which an authority is valid may be limited; and the recipient of orders at one level may have his own field for authority. But within these limits, the giving and taking of orders, having someone tell someone else what to do, is an essential part of the mechanism by which organizations function.

The giving and taking of orders might be termed *personal* authority; there is also another mode of allocation which might be called *impersonal* authority, through codes of conduct which prescribe what each member of the organization is to do under a variety of possible circumstances. The legal code is an outstanding example of impersonal authority. Since personal authority cannot be everywhere, the establishment of impersonal authoritative codes is a necessity. But it may supplant as well as supplement personal authority, having the advantage of greater predictability, along with the disadvantage of lesser flexibility.

In what follows, I shall refer primarily to personal authority; but many of the remarks will also be applicable to the impersonal variety.

The role of authority does vary among organizations. The military is the extreme case, in which authority is all-pervasive and essential. The state also exemplifies authoritative behavior in relation to its citizens, particularly with respect to police and legal control. The state shares with firms a more limited kind of authoritative control over employees. Indeed, as Herbert Simon has emphasized, an employment contract is precisely a contract on the part of the employee to accept authority. It differs therefore from a contract to purchase a commodity; what is bought and sold is not a definite objective thing but rather a personal relation. Within the scope of the contract, the relation between employer and employee is no longer a market relation but an authority relation. Of course, the scope of this authority will usually be limited by the terms of the contract, and, more fundamentally, it is limited by the freedom with which an employee can leave the job. But since there is normally some cost to the exercise of this freedom, the scope of this authority is not trivial.

Among the large organizations of our society, authority is perhaps weakest among the professions. Here, codes of ethics and standards of conduct imposed by social pressures tend to displace the more overt forms of personal or even of impersonal authority. Professional organizations have only limited and exceptional power over their members, and then only in cooperation with the state, as in disbarment; they may and frequently do, however, help in controlling entry. It is not surprising, perhaps, that universities, which have grown to have a curious mixture of educational functions, where authority is traditional though questioned, and professional concerns, should have special difficulty in defining the internal role of authority.

When conditions are stable, the role of authority, as indeed that of any other continuing social institution, is taken for granted and is little questioned. To some extent, no doubt, the acceptance of all authority is a transfer from the supreme Authority of religious belief. Marc Bloch has shown the sacred character of medieval monarchy; and religious sources as diverse as the Talmud and the Bhagavad Gita add religious sanction to the role of authority. The decline of religious belief, the "ebbing tide of faith" which Matthew Arnold could already see a century ago on the beach at Dover, may in part lie behind the decline of authority in the current world, a development deplored by some and exulted in by others. But perhaps it would be better to say that the religious and secular authority stem from the same roots and parallel each other; the structure of heavenly government mirrors that of Earth as well as supporting it. God is King in the Judeo-Christian religious language; the metaphor loses some force in a democratic age.

In eras when authority or at least specific authorities have been questioned, there is more tendency to examine the roots of and need for authority. The owl of Minerva flies not in the dusk but in the storm. Then it is argued that authority is necessary for the functioning of human society or at the very least useful for it, Hobbes's "war of each against all" being brought up as the horrible alternative. The locus of authority may shift from sacred individuals to impersonal principles, as in the English and American revolutions of the seventeenth and eighteenth centuries, or from impersonal principles to charismatic leaders, as in the fascist movements of the twentieth century, but in each case, a need for authority is perceived and raised to the level of social consciousness.

But precisely in such times of disturbance a counteracting tendency is manifest. The challenging of authority may lead to a reassertion of its importance, even to its hysterical exaltation, at one extreme, or to its complete denial or disregard, at the other extreme of antinomian and anarchistic tendencies. But a moderate response is an assertion of the need for *responsibility*, for systems in which authority performs its functional role but is subject to corrective action by its subjects. Authority will, after all, be often wrong. The need for checks, for holding the exercise of power to account, is clearly perceived. Certainly, the Anglo-American tradition is permeated with suspicion of those in authority. The past few years have seen even more distrust than usual. In fact, methods for some kind of control over political authority, both personal and impersonal, have evolved: elections, referenda, division of authority (legislative versus executive, federal versus state and local), a limited degree of judicial control, normally negative rather than positive in form, and of course the age-old methods of civil disobedience and violent rebellion.

Despite these techniques, there is still widespread dissatisfaction with the degree to which political authority displays responsibility. The government is widely perceived to be "impersonal" and remote, far from the average individual. If the democratic ideal were achieved, the electorate would be the authority; but it might well be as inadequate and irresponsible as any other. But in fact, elections have intrinsic shortcomings as a means of achieving responsibility. By their very nature, elections cannot differentiate among the myriad of specific issues but rather make decisions on a sort of average. Further, the process must of necessity be simplified, if only to keep the informational costs to the average voter within reason, so that the number of alternatives considered must necesarily be greatly reduced. The choice of presidential candidates in 1968 had little to do with the range of issues confronting the country; while the elections of 1964 and 1972 undoubtedly offered "a choice and not an echo," one can hardly feel that the full multidimensional complexity of the alternatives available to us was more than hinted at.

However, the strongest demands for imposing responsibility upon authority have arisen in extra-governmental organizations—churches, universities, and corporations. The evolution of attitudes towards corporate responsibility is an interesting combination of changes in descriptive analysis, normative attitudes, and the underlying institutional structure itself. Some fifty years ago, it became widely recognized that the nominal responsibility of corporations to their stockholders was in good part fictitious. Just about the time this viewpoint became the standard orthodoxy, its implications for the behavior of management were in fact falsified by the emergence of the take-over bid and the conglomerate—developments which exemplify the supercession of formal authority by a derivative form of the price system. The question of responsibility to stockholders has now given place to more radical demands for responsibility to other members of the firm—the workers and the customers. For a long time now, labor unions have to some extent altered the structure of authority within the firm through grievance committees and work rules. Many leftist critics, for the most part with little direct association with labor, feel that this process has not gone nearly far enough, that the conditions of work and the nature of the authority relations in working activities themselves produce personal and social distortions. Even more attention is paid currently to consumer control and to internal responsibility for product quality and for the effects of the product on others.

But all these demands for increased responsibility are bitterly resisted. It is perhaps elementary that those holding authority should resist diminution of their freedom to act. But opposition to change is not limited to those in power. Many of those over whom authority is exercised raise the strongest voices for the *status quo*. Among university faculties and Catholic parishioners, the erosion of presidential or papal authority encounters strong resistance and surprisingly little active support. There is a widespread feeling that authority is needed. In intellectual circles as well as in Middle America, it is common to diagnose the troubles of our times as due to the decline of authority; and measures to increase the responsibility of authority are always perceived as decreases in its role. Consider for example the succession of votes in most communities adverse to the creation of a civilian review board for police behavior; Philadelphia was exceptional in this regard, but the subsequent election of a former police client as mayor shows the aberrant nature of that vote. We have also seen the negative popular view, articulated by president Nixon toward judicial decisions which review and control police behavior in arrests.

In the remainder of this chapter, I want to explore further the possibilities for increasing the responsibility of authority in the large organization. There are, it would appear, five main issues: the value of authority to the organization, the conditions for its recognition, the value of responsibility, the conditions for its achievement, and, in view of these four considerations, the possibilities for achieving a reasonable trade-off between authority and responsibility.

2. The value of authority

The arguments for the value of authority are simple and familiar. They have been stated in classic though extreme form by Hobbes with regard to the particular case of government. In the absence of authority, there is a "war of each against all," and, as a result, "the life of man is poor, nasty, brutish, and short." The kernel of truth in Hobbes's argument can be put more generally, if much less dramatically, for all organizations: authority is needed to achieve a coordination of the activities of the members of the organization.

A more technical and complete restatement is useful. The generalized Hobbes argument presupposes two elements: the superior productivity and complexity of joint production, and the cost of interchanging information. Let me elaborate still further, into a series of four propositions:

1. Since the activities of individuals interact with each other, being sometimes substitutes, sometimes complements, and frequently compete for limited resources, joint decision on the choice of individuals' activities will be superior to separate decisions.

2. The optimum joint decision depends on information which is dispersed among the individuals in the society.

3. Since transmission of information is costly, in the sense of using resources, especially the time of the individuals, it is cheaper and more efficient to transmit all the pieces of information once to a central place than to disseminate each of them to everyone.

4. For the same reasons of efficiency, it may be cheaper for a central individual or office to make the collective decision and transmit it rather than retransmit all the information on which the decision is based.

Thus, authority, the centralization of decision-making, serves to economize on the transmission and handling of information.

The purest exemplar of the value of authority is the military, and of course in many respects the military has in fact been the initial organization which has grown into the state. Under conditions of widely dispersed information and the need for speed in decisions, authoritative control at the tactical level is essential for success.

A homelier example is that of traffic control. Here again the superior efficiency of authoritative control is clear. But another element is introduced. Impersonal control, the traffic signals and the signs, is more efficient than personal authority, particularly in a world where individual policemen exerting discretionary traffic authority have such high value in alternative uses.

The polar alternative to authority would be consensus. (We are of course talking about contexts in which the price system is not viable or at least does not satisfy the conditions which would make it operate at its ideal best. We may take the very existence of an organization with a need for coordination as evidence of the infeasibility or at least inefficiency of the price system.) By consensus I understand any reasonable and accepted means of aggregating individual interests. As is well known, there are deep paradoxes connected with any form of consensus mechanism, such as majority rule, short of the situation where unanimity obtains. But these problems have been explored elsewhere.

When would consensus be an adequate substitute for authority? An organization whose members have identical interests *and* identical information will be one in which spontaneous consensus would be efficient; each member would correctly perceive the best decision according to his interests, and since the interests are in common, they would all agree on the decision. In face-to-face groups, it may be possible to interchange information cheaply enough so that the identity of information can be achieved, and if the group has a sufficiently overriding commonly valued purpose, the identity of interests may also be a valid assumption.

When either interests or information differ among the members of the organization, the costs of achieving consensus rise, and hence the value of consensus as a mode of organizational decision-making declines relative to that of authority. There is space here for only a few remarks. The case where information is the same for all but interests differ is of course the classic case of social conflict and its resolution by bargaining. Despite the vast literature in this area including the rich theoretical development of the theory of games, we are far from a good understanding. It is certainly clear that the process of bargaining can itself be a very costly one, especially when the successive offers and threats take place not in the play world of recontract but in the real world of economic ruin and the savage destruction of human lives in war.

The achievement of consensus in the case where underlying interests coincide but information differs has some parallels with that of differing interests. Certainly the expressed preferences for social actions will differ among individuals in this case just as in that of differing interests. The situation is however somewhat different in that each is aware that others are trying to act in the common interest, though based on different information. If information could be exchanged costlessly, there would be no problem of arriving at a consensus. Hence, the aim in designing institutions for making decisions should be to facilitate the flow of information to the greatest extent possible. As has been seen in earlier chapters, this involves the reduction of the volume of information while preserving as much of its value as possible. To the extent that reduction of volume is accomplished by reduction in the number of communication channels, we are led back to the superior efficiency of authority.

3. *The achievement of authority*

Let me return to the notion of authority. We have asked what its function is, that is, what values it achieves for the organization. But from the viewpoint of economic theory, the value of authority is no guarantee of its existence and viability. Only in the presence of a smoothly working ideal price system is it true that needs are matched by deeds. But an organization is, I have argued, precisely a means of handling social functions when the price system fails.

It is common to argue that authority stems from control over some means of power. Within the firm, the sanctions which authority can use are basically those of hiring and firing. The state employs the sanction of the criminal law. At one level of analysis, this is a suitable answer. These sanctions do operate, and decisions by authority are obeyed in part because of the punishments that might otherwise ensue. But I would argue that it is not in fact a sufficient explanation of obedience to authority even at the immediate level; and, more important, it is not a sufficiently deep one. Let me take these points up in turn.

First, the existence of sanctions is not a sufficient condition for obedience to authority. Clearly, if enough workers disobey orders, they cannot be enforced. I am assuming, remember, that the organization is sufficiently isolated so that replacement of workers is costly. The firm simply cannot afford to fire them all. This is of course the basis for the social innovation of the strike. Similarly, a criminal law cannot be enforced if it is sufficiently disobeyed. The failure of the prohibition of alcoholic beverages is a famous example, repeated currently in drugs, gambling, and prostitution. In some cases, as in that of pornography, the authorities recognize their impotence against all but the worst excesses; in others, they maintain a costly attempt at enforcement, which results in an irregular tax on illegal activities.

One can multiply such examples, but the point is clear. It is not that authority is not in fact usually exercised; it is that the control mechanisms, the sanctions we usually think of as enforcing authority, cannot be the sole or even the major basis for acceptance of authority. Employees follow instructions, and citizens obey the law to a much greater extent than can be explained on the basis of control mechanisms.

The matter can be put in slightly more economic terms. An organization has a structure of rewards and punishments to facilitate the operations of authority. These structures are an internal version of the price system. But I am suggesting that they account only in part for the extent to which authority is in fact exercised.

Indeed, if this were not so, the exercise of authority would not be viable. Control mechanisms are, after all, costly. If the obedience to authority were solely due to potential control, the control apparatus would be so expensive in terms of resources used as to offset the advantages of authority.

The possible policy of increasing the police or other similar enforcers of sanctions raises the second objection to the hypothesis that authority depends ultimately on sanctions. As a Latin poet once asked, "Who will take care of the caretakers?" The control mechanisms are themselves organizations, composed of people. Their use to enforce authority is itself an exercise of authority. Even the most absolute dictator requires that the secret police follow orders in purging opponents. He cannot do the job himself.

Ultimately, it seems to me, authority is viable to the extent that it is the focus of convergent expectations. An individual obeys authority because he expects that others will obey it. This is obvious enough as a motive for obedience to the law because it is expected that the police will enforce it, but from what I have stated there is more to it than that. Traffic laws and in particular signal lights may be obeyed because it is clearly worthwhile to have a system in which everybody obeys them. That is, the functional role of authority, its value in making the system work, plays a part, though only a part, in securing obedience. This functional role will only be influential if in fact the authority is visible and is believed to be respected by others.

It may therefore be important to make authority visible, so that it serves as a coordinating signal. This is perhaps why external symbols surround authority—the sacred character of medieval monarchy already noted, the courtlike atmosphere around the president, the elevated bench and robes of the judge. As Lear saw clearly through his madness, "a dog's obeyed in office."

The emphasis on convergent expectations as the source of authority implies its fragility. Indeed, one can point to startling changes where the collapse of long-established authority swiftly followed recognition that it was no longer authoritative. But there is a countervailing force. The expectations that authority will be obeyed are not only of value to the maintenance of authority, but they also reduce uncertainty for those subject to the authority. The pressure to restore authority or create new authority is very strong indeed.

4. *The value of responsibility*

I write here of the functional value of holding authority responsible, the value in terms of achieving the organization's goals. There are other arguments against irresponsible authority, the effects on the worth and development of the individual human beings involved. Being subject to an authority against whom there is no recourse leads to a loss of self-respect and an atrophy of autonomous behavior; and as Acton's famous remark reminds us, the holder of irresponsible authority pays a price too. Thus, even if responsibility were deleterious to organizational function, there would be a case for introducing it in terms of individual values. But here I confine myself, in accordance with the general aim of these pages, to the value of responsibility in terms of the organization's own goals.

The basic deficiency of irresponsible authority from the

functional viewpoint is the likelihood of unnecessary error. Error, of course, there must be in a world of uncertainty. Error is unnecessary when the information is available somewhere in the organization but not available to or not used by the authority.

The reason for this failure is, simply enough, the overload of the information and decision-making capacity of the authority. In an organization of any complexity, an individual or a small group simply cannot be aware of all that is relevant. Even if formal provision is made for the acquisition of information, as in the massive provision of statistical services in the modern advanced state, no small group of individuals can assimilate the data needed.

Impersonal authority, in the forms of codes of law or conduct, is in general even less capable of making use of a flood of information. Impersonal rules cannot be adequately responsive to the large variety of possible events. To avoid misunderstanding, let me make clear that I am not asserting, as is sometimes done, that formal rules can take no account of varying circumstances. Rules can and should be formulated in a conditional form as *strategies*, to use the terminology of the theory of games. The rule should have the form, "do A if event X ocurs, B if event Y occurs, and so forth." Thus, the form of the rule incorporates the possibility of using information. But there are two vitally important limits to achieving full flexibility in the formation of rules:

1. Drawing up rules to take care of all possible relevant contingencies is itself highly costly in terms of effort and in particular of information, namely, information about the range of possible contingencies and their effects.

2. By its very nature, information is needed to implement a strategy or conditional rule. This information may be very costly, particularly if the rule has adequate complexity.

It follows that the idea of shifting from discretionary authority to rules is not the panacea it is sometimes alleged to be, particularly in the realm of economic policy.

Thus, authority, whether personal or impersonal, may be legitimately criticized, that is, others in the organization may have access to superior information on at least some matters. Cromwell reminded the Scottish authority, "I beseech you, in the bowels of Christ, think it possible you may be mistaken." Cromwell, in his turn, was not much disposed to admit the possibility that others might know enough to correct him.

The efficiency loss due to informational overload is increased by the tendency in that situation to filter information in accordance with one's preconceptions. It is easier to understand and accept information congruent with previous beliefs than to overcome cognitive dissonance. Recent political and especially military history from Pearl Harbor to Vietnam is filled with dismal and disastrous examples. To go to an earlier period, when the *Titanic* began to broadcast for help, the captain of a nearby ship decided that the message must be a mistake or a hoax; it was well known that the *Titanic* was unsinkable. In another realm of decision-making, a distinguished psychologist friend of mine has told me that the evidence for telepathy was stronger than that for many propositions accepted among psychologists; yet no one of scientific standing would take it seriously (he didn't either). These examples are not perversities; the filtering of information so that only those bits with high prior probabilities are accepted is a rational response when the volume of information exceeds the limited capacity to process it.

Thus, authority may be wrong in contexts where a corrective mechanism is potentially viable.

I have emphasized the overload factor in arguing that holding authority responsible is valuable to an organization. There is a second, more disputable, argument to the same end: that the sense of dealing with an absolute, irresponsible authority may be damaging to the performance of subordinates. This proposition received great support in the 1930s from the work of Elton Mayo and his colleagues, giving rise to the so-called human relations movement, and is something of a cliche today. But contemporary with Mayo's work was Erich Fromm's *Escape from Freedom*, which emphasized man's psychological craving for authority. I retreat from discussing such large issues in detail; in any case, the empirical evidence, such as it is, points to very little relation between the morale of workers and their performance.

5. *The achievement of responsibility*

Not only is it possible to achieve responsibility of authority, but in fact it is hard to imagine an organization in which some element of responsibility does not exist, at least in the long run. In the first place, every real organization is of limited scope. Hence, as Hirschman has stressed, exit from an organization is always possible, though possibly at considerable cost. Ultimately, an authority can be held to account by the disappearance of his organization through the exit of its members. If the customers of an organization are considered to be among its members, then the classical economic view of competition as a regulator of authority can be regarded as a special form of exit.

Apart from the drastic sanction of exit, most organizations have ways, even if not set down formally, for setting some limits on the scope of authority. Disobedience to orders, organized or unorganized, frequently sets limits to authority; and, like many other sanctions, the fear of such disobedience will constitute an internalization of responsibility.

Further, individuals exercising authority may be and are removable even in the absence of legal means. Revolution is an ever-present possibility, and, in mild forms, can occur in a wide variety of organizations.

But neither exit nor deposition are particularly satisfactory mechanisms for increasing the flow of information to organizational decision-making. The fact of exit or revolution is no doubt information that something is amiss, though it may not be at all clear what it is; and deposition implies replacement by a new authority with different sources of information. But there is nothing systematically optimal about the way new information appears.

Most modern organizations have indeed implicitly recognized the need for systematic provision of responsibility and have embodied constitutional means of achieving it. Without attempting to be exhaustive, we list some class of responsibility mechanisms:

1. Responsibility to a higher active authority, e.g., division managers to presidents of corporations. At best, of course, devices of this type merely relocate the problem.

2. Responsibility to an occasional authority. Examples are the relation of a corporation president to his board of directors or stockholders, a democratically elected official to his electorate. The responsibility is to another authority, but one which exercises its authority only through the selection of authority. Information beyond that available to the main authority is introduced, but only in a periodic maner.

3. Responsibility to a special authority valid for a limited domain. The primary example is judicial authority; the executive and the legislature are responsible to the judiciary in certain specified dimensions, such as the limits of their decision-making range or the appropriateness of their procedures, but not in others, in principle not for the substance of their decisions.

4. Responsibility to nonauthoritative groups, e.g., commissions of inquiry, ombudsmen. The responsibility in the last case is solely one of justifying the decision in terms of information available to the authority and of receiving the further information supplied by the nonauthoritative agency.

6. Consideration on the trade-off between authority and responsibility

There is much to be done in the design of institutions to reconcile the values of responsibility and authority, and only a few preliminary remarks can be made here. To serve its functions, responsibility must be capable of correcting errors but should not be such as to destroy the genuine values of authority. Clearly, a sufficiently strict and continuous organ of responsibility can easily amount to a denial of authority. If every decision of A is to be reviewed by B, then all we have really is a shift in the locus of authority from A to B and hence no solution to the original problem.

To maintain the value of authority, it would appear that responsibility must be intermittent. This could be periodic; it could take the form of what is termed "management by exception," in which authority and its decisions are reviewed only when performance is sufficiently degraded from expectations; or it could take the form of review and deeper study of a random sample of decisions or periods. No doubt all forms of these are needed for different purposes. To be effective, all of these will need complementary changes in the information system, for example, in the justification of decisions and in the specification of what they are in fact expected to achieve.

I would like in particular to urge experimentation with review groups to which specific charges of errors can be referred. To open the machinery to complaints provides an important means of tapping sources of information outside the authority. I assume such a review procedure can be arranged so that significant resources are used only for significant questions. The main function of a review group is the generation of information and its dissemination to the relevant parts of the organization. Dissemination here must mean "effective dissemination;" there must be some means of insuring that the information supplied by the review procedure is effectively used by the authority and not disregarded. I see no way of insuring effectiveness save by giving some element of authority to the review group.

A question such as this arose in the context of university governance at Harvard University. There was broad agreement on a need to define more sharply the appropriate codes of behavior for faculty and students, as a consequence of the disturbances at the University. But there was a countering demand that the behavior of the administration should be similarly accountable. A faculty committee prepared a set of resolutions which included an announced obligation on the part of the administration to be responsive to complaints and to consider seriously requests for changes in decisions and in procedures. A commission of inquiry was proposed to receive complaints and exercise some rather vague powers of reviewing them. The faculty rejected this proposal, weak as it was, on the ground that it would impede administrators in the exercise of their authority.

Clearly, there is no consensus on the need for responsibility and certainly not on its scope or on the mechanisms for its achievement. But the unthinking acceptance of authority based on echoes from religion and kingship is, I believe, gone. Even the acceptance of the popular will as reflected in majorities is weakened, as is shown by the widening acceptance of civil disobedience. In any case, majority rule is no model for organizations with functionally differentiated elements among its membership, such as firms or universities. Authority is undoubtedly a necessity for successful achievement of an organization's goals, but it will have to be responsible either to some form of constitutionally planned review and exposure or to irregular and fluctuating tides of disobedience.

References

Arendt, H. 1970. *On Violence*, Part II. New York: Harcourt, Brace & World.

Arrow, K.J. 1963. *Social Choice and Individual Values*, 2nd ed. New Haven: Yale University Press.

Arrow, K.J. 1971. *Essays in the Theory of Risk-Bearing*. Chicago: Markham, and Amsterdam and London: North-Holland. Chapters 4, 5, 8, 9, and 10.

Banfield, E.C. 1958. *The Moral Basis of a Backward Society*. Glencoe, Illinois: The Free Press.

Becker, G.S. 1964. *Human Capital*. New York: National Bureau of Economic Research, 18–29.

Bloch, M. 1924. *Les rois thaumaturges*. Strasbourg: Librarie Istra.

Fromm, E. 1941. *Escape from Freedom*. New York and Toronto: Rinehart.

Gombrich, E.M. 1960. *Art and Illusion*. New York: Pantheon. Especially Chapter IX.

Hirschman, A.O. 1970. *Exit, Voice, and Loyalty*. Cambridge: Harvard University Press.

Hurwicz, L. 1960. Optimality and informational efficiency in resource allocation processes. In K.J. Arrow, Karlin, S. and Suppes, P., eds. *Mathematical Methods in the Social Sciences, 1959*. Stanford: Stanford University Press. Chapter 3.

Kaysen, C. 1949. Basing point pricing and public policy. *Quarterly Journal of Economics* 63:289–314, especially 294–98.

Kornai, J. 1971. *Anti-Equilibrium*. Amsterdam and London: North-Holland, and New York: American Elsevier. Chapters 4, 5, 6, 18, 19, and 21.

Jorgenson, D.W., McCall, J.J. and Radner, R., 1967. *Optimal Replacement Policy*. Chicago: Rand McNally, and Amsterdam: North-Holland.

Marschak, J. 1959. Remarks on the economics of information. In *Contributions to Scientific Research in Management*. Los Angeles: Western Data Processing Center, University of California, 79–98.

Marschak, J. 1968. Economics of inquiring, communicating, deciding, *American Economic Review Papers and Proceedings* 58:1–18.

Marschak, J., and Radner, R. 1972. *Economic Theory of Teams*. New Haven and London: Yale University Press.

Mayo, E. 1946. *The Human Problems of an Industrial Civilization*, 2nd ed. Boston: Graduate School of Business Administration.

Miller, G.A. 1956. The magical number seven, plus or minus two: some limits on our capacity for processing information. *Psychological Review* 63:81–97.

Radner, R. 1968. Competitive equilibrium under uncertainty. *Econometrica* 36:31–58.

Raiffa, H., and Schlaifer, R., 1961. *Applied Statistical Decision Theory*. Boston: Graduate School of Business Administration, Harvard University. Chapters 1, 4.

Schelling, T.C. 1960. *The Strategy of Conflict*. Cambridge: Harvard University Press. Chapters 2, 3, and 5.

Simon, H.A. 1957. *Models of Man: Social and Rational*. New York: Wiley, and London: Chapman and Hall. Chapters 10, 11, 14, and 15.

Stigler, G.J. 1951. The division of labor is limited by the extent of the market. *Journal of Political Economy* 59:185–93.

Summers, R. 1967. Cost estimates as predictors of actual costs: a statistical study of military developments. In T.A. Marschak, Glennan, T.K., Jr., and Summers, R. *Strategy for R & D*. New York: Springer. Chapter 4.

Index

This book was typeset in Linotype Caledonia and composed by Heritage Printers, Inc. It was printed by The Murray Printing Company. The cloth-bound edition was bound by Vail-Ballou Press, Inc. and the paperbound edition by The Murray Printing Company.